● 973.33
CUN   Cuneo, John R
        The battles of
        Saratoga

1791

A summary of events which led to revolts of
colonists against Great Britain and the course of the
fighting up to the summer of 1777. Discusses Burgoyne's plan to capture Albany, his unsuccessful
attempts to break through the American lines, his
retreat to Saratoga and surrender to General Gates.
The importance of this victory, which influenced the
French to provide the Americans with men and
material, thus contributed to the eventual defeat of
the British. In concluding chapter, author tells how
he disagrees with other historians about events and
personalities of the Campaign.

THE BATTLES
OF SARATOGA

THE MACMILLAN BATTLE BOOKS ARE PREPARED UNDER
THE GENERAL EDITORSHIP OF EDWARD R. SAMMIS

THE
BATTLES OF
SARATOGA

The Turning of the Tide

By JOHN R. CUNEO

THE MACMILLAN COMPANY, NEW YORK
COLLIER-MACMILLAN LIMITED, LONDON

MAPS BY RAFAEL PALACIOS

PICTURE CREDITS: Anburey, *Travels Through the Interior Parts
of America*, London (1789), 10–11, 30–31, 44, 76–77; Culver Pictures,
title page, 15, 20, 27, 48, 59, 70; Bob Cowan, Dallas, Texas, 62; John
R. Cuneo, 21; Fort Ticonderoga Museum, Ticonderoga, New York,
13, 33, 38, 68; The Frick Collection, 28 (right); Historical Pictures
Service–Chicago, 18–19, 22–23, 29, 40, 46, 52, 65, 80; Lezius, *Die
Ehrenkleid des Soldaten*, Berlin, 64; Library of Congress, 24, 28
(left); The Metropolitan Museum of Art (Gift of Robert W. De-
Forest, 1906), 14; National Park Service, United States Department
of the Interior, 74; New York Historical Society, New York City, 56
(left); New York Public Library (Picture Collection), 36–37; New
York State Department of Commerce, 92.
Cover photograph courtesy of Historical Pictures Service–Chicago.

To the dedicated workers in the National Park Service whose efforts to preserve and make available to the public our historical heritage in a third dimension are too often unrecognized

CONTENTS

I

THE NORTHERN INVASION

IT WAS a cocky, self-assured column of British redcoats marching through the woods just south of the head of Lake Champlain that bright July day in 1777.

They had reason to feel cocky. Fort Ticonderoga, the "impregnable" bastion guarding the waterway leading to New York, where General William Howe's troops faced General Washington's Continental Army, had just fallen to the invading British Army, practically without firing a shot.

The American defenders of the fort had retreated south in confusion. The column—116 men of "The Fighting Ninth" under Lieutenant Colonel John Hill—had been sent to follow and harry the disorganized units. Perhaps the Americans were planning to make a stand at Fort Edward on the Hudson River. Essentially a reconnaissance-in-force, Hill's troops nevertheless were ready to attack in order to keep the Americans off balance.

By nightfall the Americans had occupied Fort Anne, a decaying wooden palisade in the wilderness. The British camped a short distance away, confidently looking forward to a quick assault in the morning which would send the Americans scurrying farther south toward Fort Edward.

Instead, at dawn on July 8, a throng of Americans burst from Fort Anne and charged the British camp. The British fell back to the summit of a nearby hill. There Colonel Hill re-formed his lines, and sent for reinforcements.

Now the British stood firm. For almost three hours the redcoats grimly held their ground in the face of repeated American attacks. Finally the Americans' ammunition began to give out and they left the field. After pausing

briefly to set fire to the rotting timbers of the fort, they withdrew. Rain poured from the heavens, putting out the fire and adding to the discomfort of the retreating soldiers. The rear guard peered backward: where were the British?

Reinforcements had reached Hill, but they brought him orders from the commander of the invading army, "Gentleman Johnny" Burgoyne, to pull back. The pursuit was to be abandoned. To the astonishment of the tired American soldiers limping into Fort Edward, the British advance had jolted to a complete halt.

In the interval between the fall of Fort Ticonderoga and the battle near Fort Anne, General Burgoyne had decided that he should advance no farther without moving his matériel—artillery, ammunition and provisions—into

A view of the saw-mill and blockhouse near Fort Anne

the vicinity of Fort Edward. He made up his mind to use
two routes: by water down Lake George (with a short
land portage) and by land from Fort Anne.

The resulting delay gave the Americans an ideal opportunity to reorganize and make life difficult for Burgoyne.
The American commander of the Northern Department,
General Philip Schuyler, knew that the road from Fort
Anne led through dense woodlands, over bogs and swamps
and through numerous ravines. Under Schuyler's orders,
the Americans felled trees across the roads and diverted
streams to wash out the roadbeds, making the most of
what nature had already done to hamper the British.

Aftermath of Ticonderoga

The fall of Fort Ticonderoga was not—as the British,
and indeed, many Americans believed—an indication of
an American lack of spirit. A mountain towered above
the fort a short distance to the southeast. The Americans
in command had not believed that artillery could be hauled
up its steep slopes. But when they saw British guns on the
summit of the mountain, they knew that the fort could
no longer be defended. The fort's commander, General
Arthur St. Clair, had made the decision—no matter what
blame the move might bring down on his head—to retreat.
Burgoyne could not be halted here, but if the defending
army was saved, it would have an opportunity to stop the
British advance elsewhere.

The loss of the famous fort blinded the Continental
Congress to the brighter side of the picture. It was both
thunderstruck and angry. Samuel Adams wrote that it

General Philip Schuyler

was "difficult to account for Evacuation of these Posts even on the Principle of Cowardice." John Adams wrote his wife: ". . . We shall never defend a post until we shoot a general."

At Washington's headquarters the reaction was the same. Alexander Hamilton wrote: "All is mystery and dark beyond conjecture." Washington informed General Schuyler that he was "chagrined and surprised." No one seemed to realize that St. Clair had rescued the principal American asset: the Northern Army.

The British were jubilant at the fall of Ticonderoga. Loyalists had been calling the year (1777) "the year of the hangman," alluding to the gibbet-shape of the numeral "7." Now more than ever they were sure that the rebel leaders would soon be swinging by their necks. King George himself is said to have run into the Queen's dressing room on receipt of the news, shouting "I have beat them! I have beat all the Americans!"

The attention of both sides, previously centered around New York City and nearby New Jersey, where the con-

General Arthur St. Clair

tending armies under Howe and Washington had been sparring, now was focused on the North. Was the fate of the American revolt to be determined in the wilderness of northern New York, where the invasion from Canada was starting to sweep everything in its path?

Rebellion into Revolution

When Great Britain had emerged in 1763 as victor in the struggle with France for North America, its colonists seemed loyal and contented subjects. What had happened to cause them to be facing the same government with ready muskets twelve years later?

The origin of the revolt was undoubtedly the fear of some colonists that Parliament was threatening the unusual liberty of action which had been the Americans' heritage from the beginnings of the settlements in the wilderness. Political theorizing concerning the limits of Parliament's power turned into fiery emotional appeals which brought angry mobs into the streets. Law and order were flouted. These challenges were met by reprisals which only hardened the colonists' determination to protect their prized "liberty and property." An armed clash became inevitable.

Not all Americans were affected. Many would not turn against the mother country no matter what the provocation. Others felt that there was no provocation. Some sought to remain neutral. How many were Loyalists (or Tories), neutralists or Patriots (to give the rebels the title won by virtue of their eventual victory), will never be known.

Finally, in April, 1775, fighting began: skirmishes occurred at Lexington and Concord between local militia and British troops seeking rebel artillery and military stores. Aroused, an angry countryside turned the British withdrawal to Boston into a disastrous retreat. Overnight an American army took the field and challenged the British.

Independence became the only alternative when the rebelling colonists realized that both King and Parliament

April 19, 1775: The struggle at Concord Bridge

were united against them to establish the supremacy of Parliament. On July 4, 1776, the representatives of the protesting Americans took the step in their historic Declaration of Independence. The rebellion had become a revolution.

The Call to Arms

Without victory on the battlefield the Declaration of Independence was only a scrap of paper. Could the loosely organized states turn out an army able to defeat the British?

The first challenge came in the Colony of Massachusetts Bay, where the revolt was most popular. The general reaction to the British "invasion" of Concord supplied a ring of enthusiastic citizens who continued to hold the royal forces in virtual captivity within Boston. The stubborn resistance of the colonists to repeated British attacks at the battle of Bunker Hill gave the lie to the stories of American cowardice popular in the British press.

The British felt that their red-coated army was the best in the world. But there were serious weaknesses beneath its brilliant exterior. It had a defective organization and poor administration. It was hampered by casual officers holding rank by virtue of purchased commissions and private soldiers recruited or forced into service from the depths of humanity.

In battle all opponents feared the awesome fire power of the British line. It did not come from accurate marksmanship, but rather from the shock of united platoon firing, with ranks standing shoulder-to-shoulder, two or three deep. Opposing lines were allowed to come quite close before the redcoats pressed the triggers of their heavy flintlock muskets. ("Don't fire until you see the whites of their eyes" was a command Americans learned from the British Army.) At the order "Fire!" the massed salvo would put so much lead into the air that the shock alone would halt any but the most reckless attackers. A rapid succession of volleys would follow. If the enemy pressed on to come to grips, the British soldier knew well how to use the long, slim bayonet on the end of his musket.

The field battery of the day, manned by the Royal Artillery, took its place in the British front ranks. It fired solid cast-iron balls of various sizes (generally from three to twenty-four pounds) or grape- or caseshot. Caseshot was simply a canister or can filled with scrap, musket balls or slugs. Grapeshot was similar but with larger iron balls and no metal can. Although not accurate, the smoothbore cannon were formidable weapons in the range from 250 to 700 yards.

Morale of men and officers alike in the British Army in North America dropped when a hesitant home government and incompetent generals permitted the Americans not only to bottle the British in Boston throughout 1775 and into 1776 but to take the initiative elsewhere. Even the famed British Navy failed to give the land forces any effective support.

On the other side of the lines around Boston was the American Army of civilians. The Continental Congress quickly agreed to supply and pay the men in the lines and appointed George Washington of Virginia Commander-in-Chief.

Washington had had only limited experience as a leader in the French and Indian War of 1754–63. But he had the magic quality of leadership which men instinctively recognized. More important, the war brought out in him a stubborn pride and refusal to admit defeat. No matter how severe the immediate drubbing, Washington was always thinking of how the war could be continued on the morrow.

Outside Boston, Washington found an armed mob— untrained, ununiformed and undisciplined. He used British inactivity to good stead. He weeded out incompetent officers and men, discouraged intersectional rivalries and tried to install a British type of discipline. At the same time he was able to preserve the energy and resourcefulness which were the shining attributes of the civilian army.

General George Washington takes command of the American Army.

On June 14, 1775, the Continental Congress authorized the raising of the first units of a national army. Ten companies of riflemen—six from Pennsylvania, two each from Virginia and Maryland—each with an authorized strength of sixty-eight men, were to "join the army near Boston, to be there employed as light infantry, under the command of the chief officer of that army." The men enlisted for a year.

Making passionate appeals against a background of squealing fifes and thumping drums, recruiters quickly raised the companies. Here and there, there were more volunteers than needed: marksmanship decided who would be taken.

Newspapers followed the recruits' march to Boston almost step by step. There were descriptions of their fringed

1791

*A platoon of
American recruits
falls in
for inspection.*

tow or linen hunting frocks reaching to mid-thigh with
"Liberty or Death" or "Don't Tread on Me" painted on
them. The riflemen wore their narrow-brimmed black hats
usually cocked on the left side only, perhaps with a tuft
of deer's fur in the shape of a buck's tail waving aloft.

Everywhere they were greeted with enthusiasm. Local
militia would escort them through towns. Families would
drop what they were doing to gape at the tall men in out-
landish garb marching to Boston, or to offer them fresh
bread or cool cider.

The riflemen knew that their chief attraction was their
skill with their guns: long-barreled flintlocks developed
principally by German gunsmiths in Pennsylvania. Instead
of the smooth interior of the barrel of the musket, the
standard military gun, the rifle had ridges ("rifling") to

hold the ball tightly and to give it a twist or spin. Thus, unlike a musket ball, the rifle ball would leave the barrel in a straight line, with a spin which contributed to its accuracy and stability in flight. The Americans changed the German model by lengthening it for greater accuracy, range and velocity. Its balance was improved and its weight was lessened.

It had been found in Europe that a ball of the proper caliber wrapped in a greased patch of leather or cloth could be more easily rammed into the barrel than the

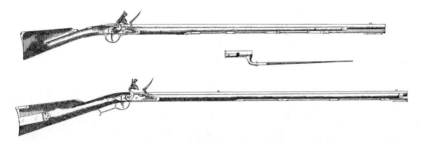

TOP: Musket and bayonet of the type used by British and Americans during the Revolution. BOTTOM: An American rifle

formerly used, slightly larger ball, which had to be forced down into the barrel, and yet there would be a tight fit. The Americans followed this system and soon there were claims of accurate shooting up to three hundred yards.

Whether the balls from the rifles or the propaganda that heralded the presence of the riflemen in the American lines around Boston had the greater effect on the British is difficult to say. In any case, the riflemen were soon known as "the shirt-tail men, with their cursed, twisted guns, the most fatal widow-and-orphan makers in the world."

The Initial Strategy of the War

At first neither side had any definite plan for winning the war. Each seemed to act on impulse. Perhaps Canada could become the fourteenth colony: the Americans sent men to drive out the weak British force stationed there. The British sent an expedition to take Charleston, South Carolina, potentially an ideal southern base of operations. Both efforts failed. Meanwhile the British Army sat in Boston and the Americans were content to hold the hills encircling the city. When the redcoats finally sailed out of Boston harbor in March, 1776, General Wash-

A long view of General William Howe's expeditionary force anchored off Staten Island in August, 1776

ington waited to see where they would strike next.

In London the government finally realized that the revolt was not going to be put down easily. Parliament authorized an army of 55,000. When enlistments in Great Britain failed to fill the ranks, the government turned to Europe for help. Various German princes sent their regiments in return for pay. Now 42,000 troops would be in America by mid-1776.

It became obvious to both sides that the British would aim at New York City. Here was a wide, deep and sheltered harbor. Here was the Hudson River stretching far to the north, forming with Lake Champlain an almost uninterrupted waterway to Canada, an ideal line of communication with the British forces there.

American troops marched from Boston to New York and began erecting forts on Manhattan Island and adjacent shores. Early in July the white sails of British ships began to appear in the harbor. They multiplied each day until 52 warships and 427 transports were swinging at their anchors. The troops—34,000—went ashore on Staten Island and campfires dotted the night as the men slapped mosquitoes, cursed the heat and waited for action.

The storm began with a well-conducted landing by the British on the extreme west end of Long Island. This was followed by a brilliant surprise attack on the unguarded American left flank, resulting in the complete defeat of the Americans in the Battle of Brooklyn on August 22. But Washington withdrew from a possible encirclement, crossing from Brooklyn to New York under the cover of

General Washington captures the British garrison at Trenton.

night and a heavy fog. The British followed and he continued to fall back.

Repeated defeats and constant withdrawals—from New York City, from New York State, across New Jersey into Pennsylvania—caused Americans to lose heart. Yet when all seemed lost, Washington appeared at dawn on the day after Christmas, 1776, on the outskirts of Trenton, then held by the German allies of the British. In a surprise attack under cover of a sleet storm, the Americans captured the garrison of more than 850 troops without the loss of a single man. When Washington followed this success by parrying enemy counterblows and inflicting heavy losses with only slight casualties on his side, Philadelphia, the seat of the American government, seemed safe. Patriot hopes again soared.

In the North a British Army under General Guy Carleton had planned to implement Howe's attack on New York City with a drive down the Richelieu River into Lake Champlain. But Carleton had to put together a fleet to transport his men and he was not ready to embark until early October.

An American "fleet" had been hastily constructed during the summer and, under the command of Benedict Arnold, it boldly sailed against Carleton. The Americans fought bravely and desperately in the Battle of Valcour Island (October 11), and although finally defeated, they had delayed the British advance. Even without the battle, Carleton was halted. He had waited too long before starting his invasion: winter was too near for him to begin a siege of the American Fort Ticonderoga. He turned back to Canada at the beginning of November.

The British Plan for 1777

In November, 1776, Sir William Howe began to look forward to operations in 1777. He planned three simultaneous offensives to paralyze the Americans in the North: one toward Boston from a newly won base at Newport, Rhode Island; another up the Hudson toward Albany from New York City; and the third southwesterly from New York City in the direction of Philadelphia, the enemy's capital. This plan would knock New England out of the war and open the road to the South. But he warned the home government that to achieve success in this operation he would require 15,000 additional troops.

Shortly before Christmas, Howe informed London that if he did not receive the desired reinforcements, he would stand on the defensive in Rhode Island and New York and take the offensive only against Philadelphia.

Howe's messages went to Lord George Germain, Secretary of State for the Colonies. In early March, Howe received Germain's answer. He would be sent only 7,500 men. Howe assumed that the cut meant approval of his December plan to attack only Philadelphia.

Meanwhile, London hailed the return of handsome General John Burgoyne from service under Carleton in Canada. Brave, acclaimed a military genius, with a flair for both the spoken and written word, "Gentleman Johnny" was admired by rich and poor, men and women alike. Some of his faults were the foibles of his age: gambling, wenching, the striking of poses in public. Few seem to have realized that his military reputation rested on exaggerated reports of a minor exploit in Portugal; his literary

American ships in action during the Battle of Valcour Island

abilities were overrated and his grandiloquence was often pompous nonsense.

When Burgoyne was stepping ashore in England, the government was considering another invasion from Canada. The King made a popular suggestion: Why not appoint Burgoyne commander? The general was asked to set down in writing his thoughts about such an invasion.

Burgoyne quickly came up with a memoir entitled *Thoughts for Conducting the War from the Side of Canada*. In it he proposed that an army of 8,000 regulars supported by artillery, Canadians and Indians move into Lake Champlain and take Fort Ticonderoga by early summer. Then the invaders would have a choice either of continuing to Albany to enable Howe "to act with his whole force to the southward," or of turning from Ticonderoga to the Connecticut River and driving south to meet Howe's invading force from Rhode Island.

Howe's December letter had arrived in London just

before Burgoyne submitted his proposal. The Rhode Island thrust was out, but Burgoyne's alternative suggestion was a push to Albany, which, he wrote, would allow Howe to move his army to the south. This was what Howe was proposing to do; the plans seemed to dovetail.

Germain read in them the promise of a British triumph in 1777. Burgoyne was named commander of the Canadian expedition. Howe was encouraged to undertake his thrust at Philadelphia, with a weak admonition to return in time to cooperate with Burgoyne. Before the members of Parliament Germain predicted victory.

The Invasion Begins

Burgoyne sailed for Quebec and arrived on May 6. He handed Germain's orders to Carleton. Burgoyne was to have the bulk of the army in Canada in order to "proceed with all expedition to Albany, and put himself under the command of Sir William Howe." American resistance was to be divided by a diversionary force under Lieutenant Colonel Barry St. Leger which would move

LEFT TO RIGHT:
General William Howe,
General John Burgoyne,
Lord George Germain

eastward along the Mohawk River from Lake Ontario.

Burgoyne's army was made up of 3,724 British rank and file (including the crack light infantry and grenadier companies of all the regiments in Canada) and 3,016 German mercenaries, also top-notch soldiers. He had an unusually large number of cannon (138) with both British and German artillerymen. There were about 250 Canadians and Loyalists. Indians came in while the expedition moved: perhaps some 400 were the highest number ever present at one time. The expedition totaled about 7,800 men.

It was a formidable force, but it had one serious deficiency. Like all armies of that time, the British lacked a military transport system. They depended on civilian help. Unfortunately, Canada lacked vehicles and draft animals. There would be trouble when the expedition had to leave the waterways to transport supplies overland.

On June 3 the expedition began to roll. The advanced corps under Brigadier General Simon Fraser moved from its winter cantonment to assemble at Fort St. John on the Richelieu River. Three days later it embarked. Now the

expedition began to move in divisions down the Richelieu.
Indians in light birchbark canoes, some holding twenty or
more warriors, glided over the water; flat-bottomed bateaux crowded with red- and blue-coated soldiers followed,
clumsy by contrast, with oars glittering in the sunlight.
Fifes, horns and drums made the surrounding forests ring.
Larger boats—gunboats, brigs, sloops crowded with the
artillery, provisions, ammunition and stores of every vari-
ety, the commanding officers and the usual complement
of civilians, male and female, who followed the armies of
that day—spread their sails. Overhead flew huge flocks of
carrier pigeons, at times blotting out the summer sun.

The main body of Indians joined the army while it
camped on the shore of Lake Champlain at the outlet of

A view of St. John's, Canada, embarkation point for the British invasion force

the Bouquet River. Burgoyne addressed them on June 21, whipping up their war spirit but at the same time trying to divert their ferocity from civilian noncombatants who might fall into their hands. Officers watching the Indians gyrating and howling madly in their war dances wondered about the efficacy of his remarks.

On June 30 the main body of the invasion force was at Crown Point, about twelve miles north of Fort Ticonderoga. Poised to march on his first main objective, Burgoyne sounded the keynote of his expedition in his orders of the day: "This Army must not retreat."

Now both by land and on the narrow arm of Lake Champlain stretching from Crown Point to Ticonderoga, British columns approached the American fort. Burgoyne's

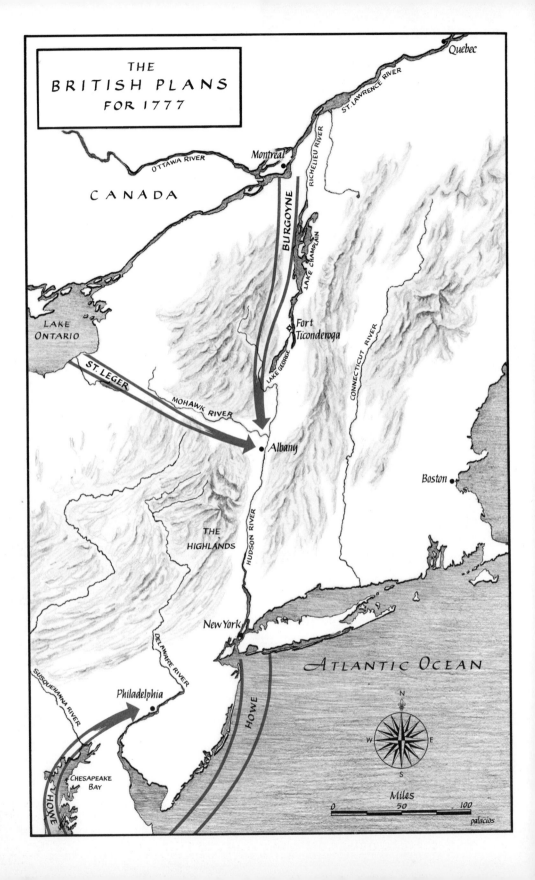

THE
BRITISH PLANS
FOR 1777

Quebec

ST. LAWRENCE RIVER

OTTAWA RIVER

Montreal

RICHELIEU RIVER

CANADA

BURGOYNE

LAKE CHAMPLAIN

Fort
Ticonderoga

LAKE ONTARIO

LAKE GEORGE

CONNECTICUT RIVER

ST. LEGER

MOHAWK RIVER

Albany

Boston

THE
HIGHLANDS

HUDSON RIVER

SUSQUEHANNA RIVER

DELAWARE RIVER

New York

ATLANTIC OCEAN

HOWE

Philadelphia

HOWE

CHESAPEAKE
BAY

N
W   E
S

Miles
0   50   100

palacios

Indians and light infantry probed for hostile outposts. Where were the American scouts?

The American Strategy for 1777

General Washington, preoccupied with the threat posed by the vast army under Howe, announced in March, 1777, that it was "against all probability" that the British would invade by way of Lake Champlain. For a while he thought Howe might be planning to go up the Hudson to attack the American forts in the steep hills lining the river ("The Highlands") about a third of the distance from New York to Albany. By the end of May, when Howe had made no move, Washington was convinced that the Delaware was the British objective. He believed that the Canadian-based forces were coming to reinforce Howe but that they were being shipped via the high seas. Consequently he made no effort to reinforce the garrison at

General Burgoyne addresses his Indian allies.

Ticonderoga, planning to concentrate all his strength to halt Howe.

The command at Fort Ticonderoga curiously made no effort to see what was happening north of the post. When a prisoner disclosed the British plans in June, he was thought only to be spreading false rumors. It was not until the British were pushing at the outposts that the garrison's commander realized what he faced. Then the fall of the fort quickly followed and the garrison began its retreat to the south. Some of the militia used the opportunity to desert.

About 4,500 Americans finally gathered at Fort Edward. But the fort was in such a ruinous state that it was difficult to believe there had been a fortification there a mere twenty years before. It was no place to make a stand.

Schuyler's army fell back down the Hudson in a series of steps. He began fortifying at Stillwater, some twenty-five miles south of Fort Edward, but changed his mind and pulled back almost to the outskirts of Albany. Where the Mohawk River met the Hudson, the road to Albany ran across several islands with shallow fording areas in between. Here the Americans would make their stand.

Meanwhile, on July 30, Burgoyne had arrived in the vicinity of Fort Edward. His men had worked miracles in overcoming the obstacles placed in their path by the Americans. But only a trickle of the British matériel sent by way of Lake George came in. There were not enough draft animals and wagons; rains had turned the roads into quagmires to slow up the few teams available.

Naturally Burgoyne took eager heed of a report that near the towns of Manchester and Bennington, in the

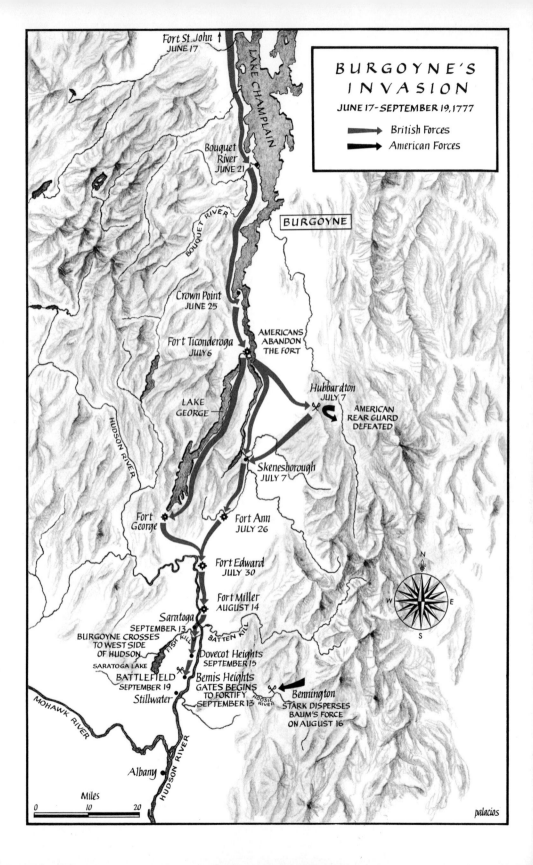

Fort St. John
JUNE 17

LAKE CHAMPLAIN

BURGOYNE'S
INVASION
JUNE 17 – SEPTEMBER 19, 1777

→ British Forces
→ American Forces

Bouquet
River
JUNE 21

BOUQUET RIVER

BURGOYNE

Crown Point
JUNE 25

Fort Ticonderoga
JULY 6

AMERICANS
ABANDON
THE FORT

LAKE
GEORGE

Hubbardton
JULY 7

AMERICAN
REAR GUARD
DEFEATED

HUDSON RIVER

Skenesborough
JULY 7

Fort
George

Fort Ann
JULY 26

N

W   E

S

Fort Edward
JULY 30

Fort Miller
AUGUST 14

Saratoga
SEPTEMBER 13
BURGOYNE CROSSES
TO WEST SIDE
OF HUDSON

FISH KILL

BATTEN KILL

Dovecot Heights
SEPTEMBER 15

SARATOGA LAKE

BATTLEFIELD
SEPTEMBER 19

Stillwater

Bemis Heights
GATES BEGINS
TO FORTIFY
SEPTEMBER 13

HOOSIC RIVER

Bennington
STARK DISPERSES
BAUM'S FORCE
ON AUGUST 16

MOHAWK RIVER

Albany

HUDSON RIVER

Miles

0   10   20

palacios

Hampshire Grants (modern Vermont), the enemy had concentrated cattle, horses and wagons as well as large magazines of provisions. He dispatched a force of about five hundred men under Lieutenant Colonel Frederick Baum to capture the supplies.

New Hampshire, realizing that the New England militia had no confidence in General Schuyler after the loss of Fort Ticonderoga, had created an independent command under General John Stark to protect its frontier against Burgoyne. By August 9 Stark was in Bennington with some twelve hundred men ready to attack Burgoyne's

flank. Baum's march saved him the trouble of moving.

Baum had penetrated deep into the hills before realizing he faced overwhelming numbers. He sent for reinforcements and was waiting for them in an encampment on a wooded hill about five miles east of Bennington when Stark attacked on August 16.

The Americans worked their way up the hill, firing from behind trees, fallen logs and rocks until they were near the enemy breastworks, and then carried them by storm. Pursuit of the few invaders who managed to escape death or capture brought the Americans into unex-

The Battle of Bennington: General Stark directs the attack against the redcoats.

pected collision with the relief party under Lieutenant
Colonel Heinrich von Breymann. For a moment the rebel
force wavered, but more Americans arrived on the scene
and turned the tide. Soon Breymann was fighting a rear-
guard action and was lucky to get back to camp. The
British losses totaled some 525 killed and missing.

This blow to Burgoyne came on top of a message from
Howe that he was going to Philadelphia. Burgoyne had
never stated that Howe was to meet him in Albany, but
now he decided that this was really what he had expected.
He wrote Germain on August 20: "I little foresaw that
I was to be left to pursue my way through such a tract of
country, and hosts of foes, without any cooperation from
New York. . . . I yet do not despair."

The brutal murder of Jane McCrea by Burgoyne's Indians

Burgoyne's confidence was soon put to another test: on August 28 he learned that the invasion of the Mohawk Valley had been given up. There would be no diversion from the west.

What should he do? Retreat or halt where he was? To him his orders were inflexible: he must advance. Should he form a flying column and make a dash for Albany? He ruled out this course of action because he lacked proper supplies and sufficient men to guard his line of communication with the camp he must leave behind. Most of his Indians had left him, using as an excuse his reproofs when one of them killed and scalped a young American woman. He believed that he could do only one thing: advance with his whole force slowly but surely to his objective, Albany.

By early September, Burgoyne had reached a point a dozen miles south of Fort Edward where the Batten Kill joined the Hudson. Here he decided to cross the Hudson, as Albany was on the west bank and the river broadened farther to the south. Heavy rains delayed him, but when the skies finally cleared, the movement was accomplished. Surveying his force, Burgoyne said with pride: "Britons never retreat!"

The Americans Change Commanders

General Schuyler was unable to wipe out the doubts aroused by the loss of Fort Ticonderoga. New England's suspicions of him grew to the point where the states were refusing to send men to serve under him. The Continental

General Horatio Gates

Congress decided he had to go, and on August 3 they named General Horatio Gates the commander of the Northern Department. Some months earlier, Gates had served briefly in this position.

Born in England, Gates had spent his adult life in the British Army on assignments in America and held the rank of major when the war with the French ended in 1763. Because his low birth and straitened resources hampered his chances for advancement, he retired from the army and moved to Virginia, where he purchased a plantation. He was with Washington when the rebellion broke out and the latter used Gates's army experience to good stead, making him a brigadier general and First Adjutant General of the American Army.

Gates had a good reputation for caring for the ordinary soldier, for organizing his troops and for building morale. His reappointment had an electrifying effect on the American soldiers. Their confidence mounted with the news of the victory near Bennington and the end of the British threat in the Mohawk Valley.

After pausing only to allow more reinforcements to come in, Gates began to march north on September 8.

Those who felt shame for the ignoble retreat down the Hudson now began to look forward to redeeming their reputation.

Gates was known to be defense-minded. Luck had given him, as a devoted assistant, an expert in fortifications. In the summer of 1776 a Polish officer named Tadeusz Kosciuszko had appeared in Philadelphia, perhaps the first volunteer in the American cause from abroad. Congress, recognizing the value of Kosciuszko's training in artillery and engineering, made him a colonel and sent him to serve under Gates in the Northern Army.

When Gates now again took command, Kosciuszko became the central figure on his staff. On September 9 the advancing Americans reached Stillwater, where Schuyler had thought of making a stand. The Polish engineer was not satisfied with it; he had found a better spot some three miles to the north, called "Bemis Heights."

Here the riverbank suddenly reared up, forming bluffs over a hundred feet in height, leaving only a narrow strip of land between the heights and the Hudson, on which the river road was built. West of the bluffs was wooded land intersected by streams running in narrow but deep ravines to the Hudson. Here and there were isolated farmhouses in small clearings. This terrain was extremely difficult to traverse. Only the river road or the Hudson itself offered ready passage. These would be guarded by cannon on the bluffs.

The British were only ten miles away in the village of Saratoga when Kosciuszko began to lay out his fortifications. The line would run parallel to the river road, northward to the edge of a gully, then follow this edge inland to a knoll near the barn of a farmer named Neilson. Here the line would turn southwest to terminate about three-quarters of a mile away in another ravine.

At first Kosciuszko started to throw up earthenworks, but they took too much time: log walls would be quicker. Trees fell and dirt flew as thousands of men swung axes, shovels and picks, sweated and swore while their officers shouted directions and drove them on. It became obvious that there was not enough time to create a continuous line of fortifications. The Americans first concentrated on the bluffs and then on a series of individual strongpoints.

Some Americans, realizing the decisive character of the impending clash, looked at the hastily built emplacements and were frankly worried.

By September 14 the British could hear the American evening guns. They had been warned that Gates was marching to attack them with overwhelming numbers. Now they prepared to advance, ready "for instant action."

Burgoyne did not dare to move only along the river road: if attacked he would be pinned against the Hudson in a thin, easily broken line. A column was swung inland to break its way through the woods. It covered the column marching along the river, but Burgoyne's forward movement was slowed to a snail's pace. On September 15 he advanced less than three miles. He halted at Dovecot Heights, where he remained a day.

On the seventeenth the British moved two miles closer. Only four miles now separated them from the Americans. With no notion of the American position or strength (he sorely missed his swarm of Indian scouts), Burgoyne knew only one course of action: to attack.

II

The FIRST BATTLE of SARATOGA

SEPTEMBER 19 dawned cold and foggy. But the river mists soon dissipated, leaving blue skies overhead.

Shortly after ten o'clock in the morning a cannon boomed in the British camp and a column of about 2,000 men under General Simon Fraser began to move down the wagon road running west from the Hudson. First came the advance guard and flankers: the few Indians remaining with the British, the Canadians, Loyalists and fifty picked marksmen. Next marched the light infantry and grenadier companies together with the battalion company of the 24th Regiment, and small detachments of artillery and German riflemen. Fraser's force was to follow the wagon road inland for about three miles and then turn southwest to cover the right flank of the center column. His was the longest march; the other columns could not advance beyond certain limits until he had reached the turning point.

*An Indian warrior
of the Revolutionary
period*

The center column under General James Hamilton with General Burgoyne—made up of the battalion companies of the 9th, 20th, 21st and 62nd regiments and six light artillery pieces—now began to move down the wagon road. However, it turned south on a road not quite two miles inland. The left column—the German Brunswick infantry regiments under General Friedrich von Riedesel with a German artillery detachment under Captain Georg Pausch —set out along the river road. It expected to strike the main American positions. The center and left columns each had about 1,100 men.

Burgoyne had a striking force of 4,200 men. His American opponents—largely Continental troops—had about 9,000.

Gates had divided his army into two wings. The left wing, under General Benedict Arnold, was made up of brigades under Generals Ebenezer Learned and Enoch Poor, and Colonel Daniel Morgan's Light Corps. Gates himself commanded the right wing: three brigades under Generals John Patterson, John Nixon, and John Glover.

General Benjamin Lincoln was off east of the Hudson, trying to drum up enough militia to strike at Burgoyne's rear.

Morgan's Light Corps was the most noted American unit. When Burgoyne's drive swept south, his advance screen of Indians had struck terror in the hearts of the American soldiers. Dread of the scalping knife and the "cursed warhoop" made it impossible to get men to venture into the woods. On the suggestion of the Continental Congress, General Washington had dispatched a corps of expert riflemen under Morgan "as a good counterpoise to the Indian. . . ."

Although there were only about 350 riflemen in Morgan's unit, Gates wanted to use them in his line of battle. However, it was generally agreed that the riflemen did not compare in battle to the ordinary soldier armed with a musket. Rifles were not equipped with bayonets; in hand-to-hand combat the rifleman was helpless. Rifles took far longer to load than muskets and they fouled rapidly, which destroyed their velocity and accuracy. They were not even good clubs, being weaker and more unwieldy than the sturdy muskets.

To make the most effective use of Morgan's corps, Gates had appointed Major Henry Dearborn to command three hundred musketmen joined with Morgan's riflemen as a light infantry unit. By mixing rifle and musket in the same ratio, he combined the accuracy of the former with the fire power and bayonets of the latter, and had the most powerful body of troops on either side.

Morgan's corps waited in the woods outside the Bemis Heights fortifications, ready to draw the first blood from the British.

The British center column advanced slowly. Bridges had to be built over gullies and ravines, and corduroy roads of logs had to be thrown over swamps to enable the artillery to pass. Then the column halted until notified that Fraser had turned southwest. Finally, at about 1 P.M., cannon gave this signal and the march was resumed.

American scouts watched the British camp and reported the enemy's movements. General Arnold urged Gates to hit the redcoats in the woods. Gates agreed, ordering Arnold to send out Morgan's Light Corps and to support him with other troops of the left wing.

Morgan's men marched on a trail leading north from "Fort Neilson" and soon were deployed in a long thin line through the woods. Some of them came into open

Colonel Daniel Morgan

fields—Freeman's farm, of some ten or fifteen acres. Several of the men occupied some abandoned cabins; others crouched behind rail fences outlining the fields.

Pickets of the British center column now cautiously approached the same fields. As they came out of the woods they were met by a burst of rifle and musket fire. Men clutched their wounds and slumped to the ground. Every officer save one was killed or wounded by the volley. The British fell back to the cover of the trees and returned the fire. More Americans came up and, faced by overwhelming odds, the redcoats gave way as the rebels advanced.

Meanwhile, General Fraser had positioned his troops on a small hill a short distance north of Freeman's farm. Hearing the sound of battle, he dispatched two light infantry companies with some auxiliaries. They rushed to the scene of action, where the van of Burgoyne's column was already deployed in line.

Morgan's men, unexpectedly bumping into this firm red wall, broke under the British massed fire and retreated into the woods in confusion. Morgan, thunderstruck, cried out to Colonel James Wilkinson, who had just ridden up: "I am ruined, by God! . . . My men are scattered, God knows where!"

For a moment the British faced no opposition. But the skirmish had halted their march. Now they were lined up on the edge of the woods north of the farm with the battalion companies of the 20th, 62nd, 21st and 9th regiments stretching from east to west. The 9th, filling the gap between Hamilton's and Fraser's forces, was ordered to defend this position "to the last extremity." Farther west, Fraser's light infantry and other units moved gradually to the east to fill the gap between the 9th Regiment and themselves.

British drums rolled, hoarse orders rang out and the red lines began a slow, measured advance across the open fields of Freeman's farm.

Meanwhile Morgan had hurried back to a hill south of the farm. Here he put a small, conical horn to his lips and blew. The eerie sound of wild turkey gobbles echoed and reechoed through the woods. The familiar "turkey call" rallied the American Light Corps. Riflemen and musketmen came pouring out of the woods; officers reorganized their companies.

Before they were ready, other American units began to march by. First came the men of the First New Hampshire Continental Regiment under Colonel Joseph Cilley, a part of Poor's brigade. On the edge of the woods the New Hampshiremen wheeled into battle line, fired a volley and charged.

A British soldier is struck down by an American officer.

Cilley's troops hit the British center held by the 62nd. The red line stood firm; under the blast of its withering fire, the Americans faltered and fell back. Major Dearborn with part of Morgan's Light Corps reached the battlefield too late to bolster the charge. He found only a defeated unit forming to march back to camp.

But other drums were heard coming from the south. Colonel Alexander Scammel's Third New Hampshire Continentals came up the wood trail. Cilley's men watched them pass, then—their spirits revived—turned and rejoined the battle. In piecemeal fashion, unit after unit left the American fortifications and marched to the scene of battle.

It was now almost three o'clock. The fighting had become general. Now and then it slackened to allow guns to cool or to be hastily cleaned out. As the American regiments came up, they would fire a volley, then charge across the clearing, only to break before the massed British fire. But now their withdrawals were no longer routs. As the redcoats pursued them, they regrouped at the edge of the woods. There they stood pat, repulsing British countercharges.

Not far behind the British line, the mounted officers of the staff were clearly visible. Climbing trees, Morgan's riflemen began to pick them off. One fell from a mount equipped with an especially elaborate saddlecloth: the riflemen were sure they had bagged Burgoyne! But it turned out to be no more than an aide.

British artillerymen and infantrymen were firing side by side. Their case- and grapeshot ripped through the foliage and helped break one American attack after an-

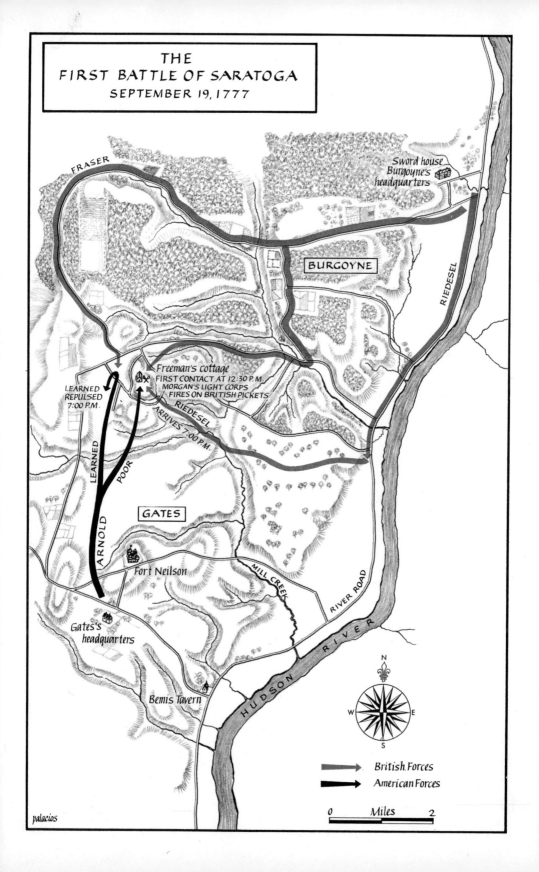

THE
FIRST BATTLE OF SARATOGA
SEPTEMBER 19, 1777

FRASER

Sword house
Burgoyne's
headquarters

BURGOYNE

RIEDESEL

Freeman's cottage
FIRST CONTACT AT 12:30 P.M.
MORGAN'S LIGHT CORPS
FIRES ON BRITISH PICKETS

LEARNED
REPULSED
7:00 P.M.

RIEDESEL
ARRIVES 7:00 P.M.

LEARNED

POOR

GATES

ARNOLD

Fort Neilson

MILL CREEK

RIVER ROAD

Gates's
headquarters

HUDSON RIVER

Bemis Tavern

N
W E
S

British Forces
American Forces

palacios

0   Miles   2

other. But exposed to the American massed fire as well as the galling scattered rifle fire, officers and men began to topple beside their pieces. The captain of one gun detachment and thirty-six out of forty-eight of his men were killed or wounded. Unmanned British guns fell silent. But the remaining artillery officers got back into action with a few men supplied by the hard-pressed infantry.

One by one, American regiments continued to arrive from the south. Their line extended farther and farther to the left. At about five o'clock Learned's brigade came up, formed into line, and tried to swing around Fraser on the British right. The move was unsuccessful.

However, American pressure was mounting. The British left was bent back in a semicircle with the 62nd holding the advanced post, exposed to fire from every side. A desperate charge pushed the Americans back for a moment. But the attack quickly lost momentum, the Americans began to counterattack and the British line seemed about to give way.

At this critical moment General William Phillips rallied the 20th Regiment, charged and forced the Americans to withdraw. The 62nd re-formed, the British line straightened. But the redcoats were thinly spread and the cannon, lacking both men and ammunition, were again falling silent. Could the British sustain another assault?

What of the British left column on the river road? Riedesel's men had begun their march south, halting to repair the road and to build bridges. Early in the afternoon they received word that a general engagement inland was imminent. Some artillery was detached to strengthen the

British troops blast the Americans at Free[illegible]m.

center column, and the remainder of the force halted. About five o'clock in the afternoon a German officer came galloping back with Burgoyne's orders to Riedesel. Riedesel was to leave a small contingent to guard the river road and march inland with the remainder of his men as quickly as possible to attack the Americans' right flank.

Riedesel was soon following a wagon trail west with about five hundred men and two six-pounder cannon under Captain Pausch. In typical German fashion the men pushed through a pine woods, shouting "hurrah" at regular intervals while the German general hurried ahead to size up the situation before he threw his troops into action.

Riedesel rode out of the woods at the eastern end of

Freeman's farm with two companies of Germans close behind. There was no time to lose: the British soldiers were in a desperate situation.

The Germans leveled their muskets. Their fire caught the Americans on their exposed right flank. Elsewhere along the battle line firing had become desultory. Hearing the crash of German muskets, the battered redcoats took heart.

Now the British cheered wildly: the main body of the German troops was coming up. Soon they were in action. Pausch's two guns were wheeled to stiffen the British line and their grapeshot pounded the Americans.

Darkness fell as the Americans were turning to answer the German salvos. Suddenly the firing ceased. The Americans shouldered their muskets and rifles, formed into columns and marched back to camp.

Pausch's cannon sent a few balls crashing into the woods after them. Then they, too, fell silent. The British and their German allies were alone on the battlefield.

III

INTERLUDE

THE Americans had come off with comparative losses: 299 killed, wounded or missing as compared to the British 556. But on the morning after the battle they peered nervously over their fortifications into the silent, fog-shrouded woods.

A British deserter had come into camp. He displayed a full cartridge box—a sign that new ammunition had been issued to the enemy's troops. American supplies were low. He warned his captors: "The grenadiers will be on you in fifteen minutes!"

But midmorning came, the fog lifted and no attack followed. Spirits rose and the men began to talk about the battle. It was "one of the greatest battles that ever was fought." The British regulars had been stopped in their tracks; maybe they would think twice before calling the Yankees "cowardly."

The Americans' confidence grew as the days went by. More men and ammunition came into Gates's camp and the fortifications were strengthened and extended.

Crisis in the American Camp

For nearly three weeks the armies remained facing each other with no action except for minor skirmishes. However, a quarrel developed in the American command which threatened to blow apart American resistance more effectively than British cannon and musket fire.

Following the battle, General Gates had hastily penned a report to the Continental Congress. In it he credited the victory to the American Army without stating that most of the troops engaged had come from the wing commanded by Benedict Arnold. Perhaps he felt that those guarding the river road had kept the British from forcing their way through at that point and deserved as much credit as those who had marched out to Freeman's farm.

At least two of the New York officers on Gates's staff still resented the fact that the general had been chosen to replace their beloved Philip Schuyler. They were openly determined to deny Gates any laurels for halting Burgoyne without any consideration of what they might do to the chances of an American victory. Arnold was shown Gates's report and his mind became poisoned with the thought that he was not mentioned because Gates was jealous and did not want him to have any credit for the victory.

Then, apparently without knowing of the trouble that was brewing, Gates issued an order on September 22 transferring Morgan's Light Corps from Arnold's wing to his own command.

General Benedict Arnold

That did it. Arnold stormed into Gates's tent. What Gates had done was clearly within the commanding general's discretion. Nevertheless, Arnold cried that he had been spurned and unjustly treated.

His manner nettled Gates, who returned insult for insult. Arnold threatened to leave the army. Gates answered that Arnold could have a pass whenever he wanted it.

Arnold stalked back to his tent and wrote Gates a long review of his complaints. He asked for a pass to Philadelphia.

Gates received the missive when he was preparing for bed; on the next morning he gave Arnold permission to leave the camp.

This simple solution of the quarrel failed to satisfy Arnold's wounded vanity. He penned another letter to Gates, finding fault with the pass and telling him that he expected an answer to his complaints. He asked for an opportunity to defend himself against the "crimes" of which he had been accused.

Gates answered with restraint: he neither had insulted Arnold nor had he made any accusations against him. He enclosed another pass, but Arnold made no move to use it.

Meanwhile, the New York officers were gleefully writing Schuyler of Gates's troubles. They created a picture of a jealous and mean-minded Gates who owed the victory entirely to Arnold, to whom he even refused reserves needed to rout the British.

These officers sought to unite the other generals behind Arnold. Rejecting these overtures, some of the generals sought to effect a reconciliation. To do so would have required some concession from Arnold, who refused and was not above daring anyone to come between him and his command.

Gates met this challenge head on. He transferred Arnold's division to his own command and appointed General Lincoln commander of the right wing. If Arnold and his New York sympathizers expected the other generals to react in his favor, they were sadly disappointed. No one even expressed any indignation with the way Arnold was being treated.

Arnold stayed on without a command. Why he did so is a mystery unless he realized that he actually had no substantial justification for leaving the camp.

Gates was often pictured as hesitant and fumbling. His maliciously applied nickname was "Granny Gates." But here he had acted swiftly and boldly. To have quailed in the face of Arnold's insolence would have torn apart the American command.

It might even have rescued Burgoyne from his critical situation.

Crisis in the British Camp

Misled by having seen the Americans leave the field, Burgoyne had planned to strike them again on September 20. When the morning light revealed the toll of the exhausting conflict, however, he changed his mind and postponed the attack until September 21.

Then another event caused him to postpone the attack indefinitely. In the predawn hours of September 21 a messenger slipped through the American lines with a letter for Burgoyne from Sir Henry Clinton. Clinton offered to attack Fort Montgomery in the Highlands "in about ten days" if Burgoyne thought the diversion would be of any assistance.

Grasping at this straw, Burgoyne immediately wrote Clinton that the diversion would draw away a great part of Gates's force. "Do it, dear friend, directly." Burgoyne told his messenger to tell Clinton that he had only thirty days' salt provisions left.

Burgoyne should have realized that Clinton's aid would come too late. It would take the messenger from eight to ten days to get his answer to Clinton. Then it would take ten days to get Clinton's expedition under way. And how much longer to break through the American forts in the Highlands? How many more days would it take to get to Albany? A month would be the minimum time required for Clinton to take Fort Montgomery.

Disregarding the fact that he could not afford to risk such a delay, Burgoyne turned from plans of an attack to constructing a series of fortifications between Freeman's farm and the Hudson. On three high points on the bluff

An eighteenth century drawing of an American light infantryman

overlooking the river he built redoubts to cover the hospital and stores piled on the bank or in the anchored bateaux. Then he built a number of small fortifications covering the British center. Near the Freeman farmhouse a strong wooden barrier was constructed which angled back to the north, covering the cottage: the "Balcarres

Redoubt," manned by light infantry under the command of the Earl of Balcarres. Behind the cottage were two small stockaded cabins held by a few Canadian troops. Then came a final fortification covering the invaders' right flank. Occupied by German troops under Lieutenant Colonel von Breymann, the redoubt bore his name.

September neared its end and Burgoyne anxiously awaited news from the south. American snipers gave his troops no chance to relax. British desertions began to increase as rumors told of the steadily mounting American numerical superiority. Then came word that the Americans had attacked the British garrisons at Fort Ticonderoga and Lake George. Although they did not take the old fort, they had cut Burgoyne's communication with Canada.

In desperation Burgoyne sent another messenger to Clinton. He wanted Clinton to tell him what to do and clearly indicated that he expected Clinton to penetrate to Albany. The messenger also was to say that if Burgoyne did not hear from Clinton by October 12, he would "retire and repass the lakes."

The end of September came and Burgoyne still had no word. Clinton had sent messengers, but they had failed to penetrate the American lines. Burgoyne gradually began to see the picture: the northern British Army was isolated in the American wilderness.

IV

The SECOND BATTLE of SARATOGA

On October 4 Burgoyne called a council of war with Generals Phillips, Riedesel and Fraser. He proposed to attack the Americans by swinging wide to the west and hitting their left and rear with practically the entire army. The meeting adjourned without the generals approving the plan.

When the generals met on the following day, Riedesel made a counterproposal: retreat. To Burgoyne's surprise and disgust, Fraser agreed with Riedesel and Phillips declined to say yes or no. Burgoyne denounced the suggestion as disgraceful.

But Burgoyne saw that he would lose control of the situation unless he modified his plan. Now he suggested a probe of the enemy left on October 7, using only 1,500 regulars and the Canadian and Loyalist contingents. The remainder of the army would guard the camp. If the

/ BÜNAU. /

Typical German soldiers who fought on the side of the British

thrust revealed any weakness, the whole army would attack on October 8. If the American position appeared impregnable, the British would retreat on October 11. His generals accepted the compromise.

On October 6 the troops received a rum ration. They knew something was up.

At the American headquarters, speculation was rife about Burgoyne's course of action. General Gates described Burgoyne as "an old gamester" who could be expected to take a wild gamble. In a letter of October 5 Gates told Washington that the British general "in a fortnight at furthest . . . must decide whether he will rashly risk at an infinite disadvantage to force my camp or retreat to his den. . . ."

Gates was ready for either move. The Americans' superiority in numbers was now staggering. Out of a grand total of 15,632 troops they had a total effective strength of about 13,065, half of whom were militia. The British army numbered 6,204 men, only 4,402 of whom were "fit for the Ranks."

On October 7, as the drums beat reveille, the British camp prepared for the attack. The company of picked marksmen and the Canadians and Loyalists would go ahead as an advance guard. About five hundred German troops from all regiments assembled to form the center of the line of advance. The light infantry came trotting up, followed by the battalion company of the 24th Regiment. They were to form the right column. Fur-hatted grenadiers lined up on the left. Finally, an artillery detachment of ten guns, both German and British, rumbled up.

The force was ready to move at about high noon. Drums rolled and orders were barked. The troops marched southeast from the British fortifications near the Balcarres redoubt. General Burgoyne was in command. At his side rode Phillips, Riedesel and Fraser.

The march was slow. Again there were delays to allow bridges for the artillery to be built over numerous gullies. After covering about two-thirds of a mile, Burgoyne called a halt. His troops sat down in a wheat field while the generals awkwardly climbed the roof of a deserted log cabin and peered south through spyglasses. They saw only the surrounding woods.

The British pause invited an attack.

American outposts near Freeman's farm had brought word of Burgoyne's approach. Gates sent Colonel James Wilkinson to reconnoiter. Wilkinson rode out, watched the British movements and turned back to report. Gates decided to repeat the strategy of the previous engagement: "Order out Morgan to begin the battle."

Morgan almost missed being on hand. He and Dearborn had gone out on October 6 with eight hundred men to harass the enemy rear. They took seven prisoners, but darkness and a heavy rain had caused them to lose their way in the woods. Luckily, they had come in early on the seventh. By noon they were ready for action.

Morgan pointed out to Gates that the British right flank now rested in a wood. The trees would afford ideal cover for the Light Corps to turn the enemy's line. Gates agreed. Then he planned to hit the enemy left (also anchored in a wood) with Poor's brigade. When the flank attacks had developed, a part of Learned's brigade would drive into the British center.

*A German officer
of the period of the Revolution*

Continentals and redcoats battle around a field piece.

Morgan, circling through the woods toward the British right, had the longest distance to go. Poor's brigade—consisting of the 1st, 2nd and 3rd New Hampshire regiments —was the first to reach the British forces. Facing Poor's men were the enemy grenadiers holding a ridge. The American officers coolly told their troops to take the first fire.

The enemy's return blast did little harm. Apparently in firing down from a height the grenadiers had aimed too high. "Fix bayonets and charge the damn rebels!" came the next order. But to the surprise of the British the

New Hampshiremen fired a volley and counterattacked.

The American fire was devastating. Wilkinson later told how "in the square space of twelve or fifteen yards lay eighteen grenadiers in the agonies of death, and three officers propped up against the stumps of trees, two of them mortally wounded, bleeding and almost speechless."

The lines clashed. Outnumbering the grenadiers better than two to one, the Americans forced them back. Now they reached the top of the ridge where the British line had originally formed. Colonel Cilley, commander of the 1st New Hampshires, jumped astride a British brass twelve-pounder, waving his sword, and ordered the cannon turned against the enemy. Another American, named Haines, was also astride a British cannon. He rammed "his bayonet into the thigh of a savage foe, recovering himself to parry the thrust of a second, and, quick as a tiger, dashing the same bloody bayonet through his head; recovering again, only to fall from the cannon, shot through the mouth and tongue. . . ."

The grenadiers continued to retreat, but contested every step.

By this time Morgan's attack on the British right flank had begun. The British marksmen and other auxiliaries were easily swept aside. The light infantry under the Earl of Balcarres wheeled to meet the flank attack and prepared to charge the riflemen. But just at that moment Dearborn's musketmen poured a raking volley into Balcarres' men and they faltered and scattered. Balcarres managed to rally his troops only with the greatest of difficulty.

Burgoyne, close to the battle lines, could see that the game was up. Not only was his advance halted, but the

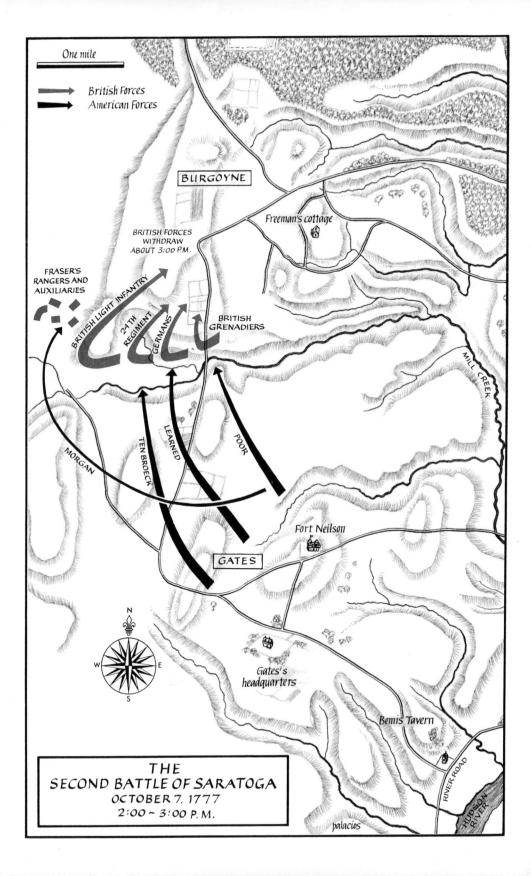

One mile

British Forces
American Forces

BURGOYNE

Freeman's cottage

BRITISH FORCES
WITHDRAW
ABOUT 3:00 P.M.

FRASER'S
RANGERS AND
AUXILIARIES

BRITISH LIGHT INFANTRY

24TH REGIMENT

GERMANS

BRITISH
GRENADIERS

MILL CREEK

MORGAN

TEN BROECK

LEARNED

POOR

Fort Neilson

GATES

N

W   E

S

Gates's
headquarters

Bemis Tavern

RIVER ROAD

HUDSON RIVER

THE
SECOND BATTLE OF SARATOGA
OCTOBER 7, 1777
2:00 ~ 3:00 P.M.

palacios

sheer weight of American numbers threatened to crush his men. Burgoyne's aides galloped out with orders to his troops to pull back into the fortified camp.

The courier to the British light infantry delivered his message. But the second aide, riding full tilt into the battle smoke, crashed into the American lines and was captured.

The regiments in Learned's brigade were advancing against the British center. Suddenly a familiar figure on horseback charged into their midst. It was General Arnold, shouting and swinging his sword. He seemed to have gone mad. (Some claimed he was drunk, others, that he was under the influence of opium. Neither explanation recognizes the explosive force of thwarted vanity.) He struck Captain Ball, one of Dearborn's men, on the head with the flat of his sword. Before the latter could defend

The Second Battle of Freeman's Farm (*painting by Chappel*)

himself, Arnold had ridden off. (The general later said that he had no recollection of the incident.)

Now Arnold was among Learned's men, urging them on against the Germans in the British center. The Germans were in a difficult situation: the retreat of the grenadiers before Poor's brigade had uncovered their left flank, and the necessity of providing their own cover had strained their resources. Learned's men fell on their front, and parts of the line gave way. The German officers managed to rally their men, however, and for a moment the line stiffened. The Americans fell back.

Meanwhile, as ordered, Balcarres had begun to withdraw his light infantry toward the redoubt at Freeman's farm. This movement uncovered the German's right flank and they had no choice but to retreat.

The Americans hung on the heels of the withdrawing British, threatening to turn the retreat into a rout. General Fraser gallantly led elements of the light infantry and of the 24th Regiment in a desperate charge to relieve the pressure. Suddenly he fell, mortally wounded by a shot fired from a tree by an American rifleman.

At the same time a tidal wave of American reinforcements—General Abraham Ten Broeck's New York militia companies, about 1,600 strong—deluged the British. The redcoats broke and fled in disorder back to their camp.

The Attacks on the British Redoubts

Flushed with their victory, the Americans were not content with possession of the battlefield. They decided to attack the Balcarres redoubt. This was no mean objective. For a distance of five hundred yards, dirt-covered log walls about twelve to fifteen feet high ran along the top of a ridge. Behind this bastion 1,500 men and numerous cannon commanded the approach. In front an abatis of sharpened logs thrust its points toward any attacker.

Late in the afternoon the signal was given for the advance. The Americans left the protection of the woods and charged across the open ground under a deadly hail of fire from the defenders. They swarmed onto the abatis, tearing at the logs and trying to climb into the redoubt. Among them was Arnold, shouting encouragement and brandishing his sword. From the protection of the log

Arnold is felled in the attack on the Breymann redoubt.

walls the defending British and Germans fired muskets and cannon at point-blank range.

The American wave broke, then formed again and surged forward. But it failed to carry the position; the British repelled one charge after another. Arnold galloped from the scene to seek a more promising part of the battlefield.

The American line had swirled around the angle and western face of the Balcarres redoubt. Beyond the Freeman farmhouse were two small stockades and, at the extreme end of the British line, the Breymann redoubt, a wall of logs about seven to eight feet high, and two hundred yards long. Burgoyne's thrust had thinned the defending forces: the stockades were held by a few Canadians, and only two hundred Germans manned the Breymann redoubt.

General Learned had begun to mount an attack on this section of the line when the American charge on the Balcarres redoubt failed. Arnold joined the rush on the stockaded cabins. The few defenders were overwhelmed with no difficulty. Now there was an opening into the rear of the Breymann redoubt and the Americans surged through it with Arnold in the van. At the same time, other Americans attacked the front of the redoubt. The numerical superiority of the enemy had robbed the Germans of any heart for fighting. When their commander fell, the last semblance of discipline vanished and they fled in disorder.

Arnold's horse was shot in the wild charge into the rear of the redoubt. He fell with it, his leg broken.

The Americans stormed into the German tents, looting and setting fire to them. The brightness of the blazes was

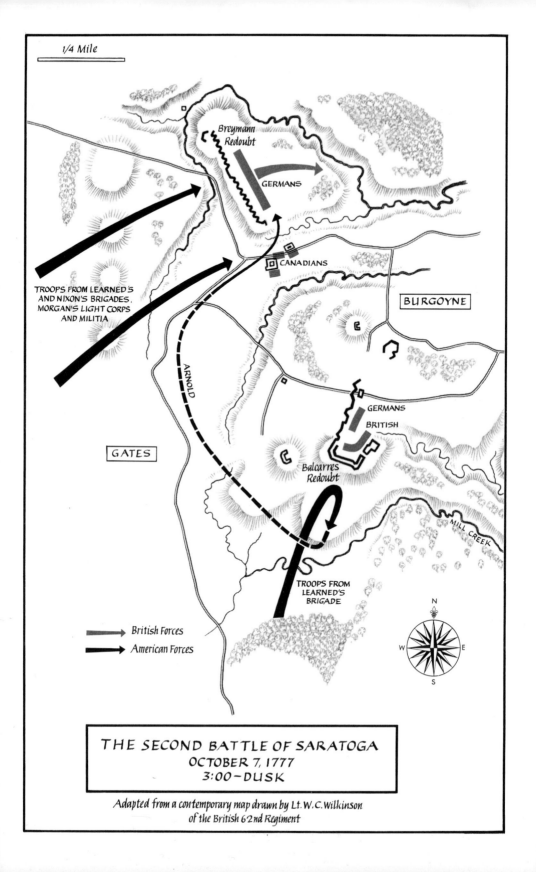

1/4 Mile

Breymann
Redoubt

GERMANS

CANADIANS

BURGOYNE

TROOPS FROM LEARNED'S
AND NIXON'S BRIGADES,
MORGAN'S LIGHT CORPS
AND MILITIA

ARNOLD

GATES

GERMANS

BRITISH

Balcarres
Redoubt

MILL CREEK

TROOPS FROM
LEARNED'S
BRIGADE

British Forces

American Forces

N
W   E
S

THE SECOND BATTLE OF SARATOGA
OCTOBER 7, 1777
3:00 – DUSK

Adapted from a contemporary map drawn by Lt. W. C. Wilkinson
of the British 62nd Regiment

a reminder that darkness had fallen. The rebels took this as a signal to pull out of the British lines.

As Burgoyne surveyed the situation he saw that the right of his camp now lay exposed to an American attack. Moreover, his troops had sustained heavy losses—600 to the Americans' 150. Hastily he drew his army back into a tight formation around his river fortifications.

Burgoyne's Retreat to Saratoga

On October 8, the day after the battle, the British prepared to withdraw. After dark Burgoyne paused long enough to bury General Fraser in one of the redoubts overlooking the Hudson. Then the retreat commenced as rain began to beat on the exhausted troops. The army hospital with its inmates was left behind.

The withdrawal was slow. The bateaux with the stores and provisions—necessary for recrossing the Hudson— had to be brought upstream against the current. The rain turned the road into mud. Burgoyne refused to abandon the artillery. Starving horses and oxen, straining to pull the guns, lost their footing in the slime. American snipers followed the British, taking a steady toll. Misery gripped the British; daily an increasing number of deserters—particularly Germans—left for the American camp.

On October 9 Burgoyne's army reached the village of Saratoga. It made camp on the north bank where the Fish Kill joined the Hudson.

General Gates had expected the British to move on. Thinking that he would be hitting only a rear guard, he planned to strike at the retreating enemy. Luckily for the

Brigadier General Simon Fraser is buried in one of the British fortifications (painting by J. Graham).

Americans, the early-morning fog lifted to reveal the muzzles of British cannon and muskets in well-prepared positions just ahead of them. The attack was hastily called off.

The area north of Burgoyne's camp was alive with Americans. On October 10 they took Fort Edward, and their numbers rapidly swelled under the command of the victor at Bennington, General John Stark.

On October 12 Burgoyne, casting discretion to the winds, issued orders for a dash northward which would have meant abandoning his artillery and baggage. The German troops were standing ready to march when the order was canceled. At the last moment Burgoyne realized that he had delayed too long. The Americans had completely ringed his camp.

Now Burgoyne's forces were under siege. The sanitation problems of masses of soldiers cooped up in a small space, dwindling food supplies, incessant enemy artillery bombardment and the British soldiers' fear of the dread riflemen, combined to make the situation insupportable.

The Convention of Saratoga

On October 13 Burgoyne held a general council of war. The council voted to open negotiations for an honorable surrender.

Early on the following morning a group of British officers and guards advanced from their lines under a white flag while a drummer beat the parley. American officers met them halfway, under the eyes of soldiers on both sides. Finally the Americans returned to camp with a blindfolded British officer. Negotiations were opened.

Officers now went back and forth with offers and counteroffers from the opposing generals. Burgoyne proposed that the British should not surrender as prisoners of war but should simply turn over their arms and be permitted to return to England. As the only condition, they would promise not to serve again in North America. On the morning of October 15 Gates agreed to the terms if surrender negotiations could be finished by 2:00 P.M. on that day and the British laid down their arms by 5:00 P.M.

Burgoyne's suspicions were aroused by the alacrity with which Gates accepted his bold proposals. Was Clinton in

Albany threatening Gates from the south? He asked for
more time; again Gates consented.

The British General's suspicions were not unfounded.
Gates was worried by Clinton's victory in the Highlands
and the discouraging reports that Albany was in danger.
(Gates's anxiety would have been increased had he known

*A view of General Burgoyne's camp on the west bank of the
Hudson River prior to the withdrawal of the British Army*

that Clinton actually had sent 2,000 men north to help Burgoyne. However, the action was taken while Gates and Burgoyne were negotiating and neither knew of it. The expedition never got very far up the Hudson.)

Nevertheless Gates had reason to be worried and he pressed Burgoyne to complete the surrender. Burgoyne—although he could only guess at what Clinton was doing—tried to stall. Finally, by late evening on October 15, the terms were settled. To the end Burgoyne tried to hide

the harsh nature of the calamity: he insisted on chang-
ing the word "capitulation" to "convention." As a London
wag later wrote:

Of Saratoga's dreadful plain—
An army ruin'd—why complain?
To pile their arms as they were let,
Sure they came off with etiquette.

On the same night a Tory came into the British camp
with a report that Gates was sending men to face Clinton,
who was probably in Albany. Burgoyne was ready to use
this move as an excuse to break the agreement. His officers,
however, saw nothing to justify further delay and forced
him to abide by the terms. On the sixteenth the "convention" was officially signed.

The surrender ceremonies took place on Friday, October 17. The thin ranks of red-coated British and blue-
coated Germans marched out of camp with drums beating.
"But," wrote a British officer, "the drums seemed to have
lost their former inspiring sounds, and though we beat the
Grenadiers March, which long before was so animating,
yet then it seemed by its last feeble effort, as if almost
ashamed to be heard on such an occasion."

No American troops except two officers were present
as unit after unit of British soldiers marched to the meadow
on the bank of the Hudson outside their camp and threw
down their guns and emptied their cartridge boxes. Then,
forming ranks again, they began their march, which
eventually was to take them to Boston, where they were
to embark for Great Britain. They passed through the
American camp where the troops were drawn up under

arms. There was no sound. "I must say," wrote the same officer, "their decent behaviour during the time (to us so greatly fallen) merited the utmost approbation and praise."

Burgoyne and his staff rode down to American headquarters. James Wilkinson, who accompanied the British, later described the scene:

General Gates, advised of Burgoyne's approach, met him at the head of his camp, Burgoyne in a rich regal uniform, and Gates in a plain blue frock. When they approached nearly within sword's length, they reined up, and halted. I then named the gentlemen, and General Burgoyne, raising his hat most gracefully, said, "The fortune of war, General Gates, has made me your prisoner," to which the conqueror, returning the courtly salute, promptly replied, "I shall always be ready to bear testimony, that it has not been through any fault of your excellency." Major General Phillips then advanced, and he and General Gates saluted, and shook hands with the familiarity of old acquaintances. The Baron Riedesel and the other officers were introduced in their turn.

Burgoyne was trying to bury the fact of his defeat in pomp; Gates was content to let the victory be his only accolade. The dinner served by the American general was in the same tenor. The table was two planks laid across empty beef barrels. There were only four plates and no tablecloth. The food was plain; the only drink, New England rum mixed with water. The two commanders had the only glasses; the other officers drank from basins.

After dinner, in the manner of a host in the eighteenth century, Gates called on Burgoyne, his guest, for a toast. Obviously embarrassed, the British general raised his glass: "General Washington."

General Burgoyne surrenders to General Gates at Saratoga.

After this toast was drunk, it was the host's turn. Gates gracefully returned the compliment: "The King."

The amenities soon came to an end. After the first burst of joy over the victory, the Continental Congress found fault with the terms of the "convention." It knew that there were troops held in Great Britain to meet any threat from the Continent. If the surrendered army was returned to England, the government would release these troops for service in America. Consequently Congress found excuse after excuse to keep the "convention troops" as virtual prisoners on this side of the Atlantic. They were shifted from place to place; they finished the war in Charlottesville, Virginia. After peace was declared, the majority never bothered to return home.

Although the Americans failed to keep their word, we now know that the British, for their part, never intended to observe the agreement. Howe sent word to Burgoyne in secret that his troops were to be brought by transport directly to New York. This was not known until more than a century later.

So, in war, honor vanishes before grim reality.

The United States Gains an Ally

The matériel of war surrendered at Saratoga was badly needed by the Americans, but it was a small gain compared to the lift the victory gave to flagging spirits. Howe's campaign to take Philadelphia had been successful and Washington had suffered reverse after reverse. By mid-October, faith in the ultimate triumph of the Patriot cause was at a low ebb.

For the first time in months hope was kindled by the good news from the north. Late on October 14 the Continental Congress heard that the British had been defeated in the second battle near Saratoga. Three days later General Israel Putnam reported from the Highlands that he had heard that Burgoyne had surrendered. The Congress voted a gold medal for Gates.

The repercussions of the victory stretched far beyond American shores. From the beginning many Americans realized that their cause could succeed only with the benefit of aid from abroad. They pinned their faith principally on France. But that nation was not so much interested in assisting dissenting colonists to obtain greater political liberty as it was in helping to dissolve the British Empire.

The Declaration of Independence was an assurance that aid to the United States would accomplish what the French desired. But without victory on the battlefield it meant nothing. France had helped but had maintained a semblance of neutrality. The setbacks in the summer of 1777 had caused France to cut its aid to a trickle and to begin to enforce its neutrality.

The Americans knew how badly they needed to get the news of Saratoga to their representatives in France. Although a rumor arrived at the end of November, the American commission awaited official word, uneasy in the certain knowledge that Philadelphia had been lost. Finally, shortly before noon on December 4 the carriage bearing the official messenger stopped outside the quarters of the commission in Passy outside of Paris. Benjamin Franklin and the others hurried to meet him: his first words were of the victory.

The report, it was said, "occasioned as much general joy in France as if it had been a victory of their own troops. . . ." Fearing it might bring a proposal of reconciliation from Great Britain to the rebelling colonists, France moved fast to forestall a truce. On January 8, 1778, the American commissioners were informed that France would enter a treaty and alliance with the United States. They, in turn, informed France that they would now reject "all propositions . . . of peace from England, which have not for their basis the entire freedom and independence of America."

The French alliance gave the thirteen Colonies the aid in men, matériel and sea power which eventually spelled the difference between victory and defeat. It also enabled the Colonies, as the United States of America, to take their place among the nations of the world.

The victories at Saratoga were responsible.

CHRONOLOGY

NOVEMBER 30, 1776. Looking forward to the British campaign of 1777 against the rebelling American colonies, General William Howe writes Lord George Germain, Secretary of State for the Colonies, that he needs 15,000 troops to carry out three simultaneous offensives against the rebels: one from Newport toward Boston, one up the Hudson from New York, one into New Jersey toward Philadelphia.

DECEMBER 26. General George Washington, Commander-in-Chief of the American forces, captures the German garrison at Trenton, New Jersey.

JANUARY 14, 1777. Germain writes Howe that he can send only about half of the requested force. Howe therefore decides to attack just Philadelphia.

FEBRUARY 28. General John Burgoyne sends a memoir to Germain entitled *Thoughts for Conducting the War from the Side of Canada.*

MAY 6. General Guy Carleton receives Germain's orders to send two expeditions from Canada, one under Burgoyne, who is to force his way to Albany, and another under Lt.-Col. Barry St. Leger, who is to make a diversion in the Mohawk Valley.

JUNE 6. Burgoyne's invasion force begins to move down the Richelieu River into Lake Champlain.

JUNE 21. The invading army reaches the mouth of the Bouquet River, where Burgoyne holds a council with his Indian allies.

JUNE 30. Burgoyne prepares to sail from Crown Point, twelve miles north of Fort Ticonderoga.

JULY 5–6. Fort Ticonderoga falls.

JULY 8. The Americans retreating from Fort Ticonderoga turn and offer stiff resistance to a British force near Fort Anne.

JULY 9. After setting fire to Fort Anne, the rebels pull back toward Fort Edward, where General Philip Schuyler, American commander of the Northern Department, has his headquarters.

JULY 10. The British advance halts to wait for artillery, ammunition, and provisions to be moved up.

JULY 21. The Americans abandon Fort Edward.

JULY 30. Burgoyne's army reaches Fort Edward.

AUGUST 3. The Continental Congress recalls General Schuyler and appoints General Horatio Gates commander of the Northern Department.

AUGUST 16. A British force under Lt.-Col. Frederick Baum is defeated near Bennington by General John Stark's militia.

AUGUST 28. On top of the unexpected news that he will have

no support from Howe, Burgoyne learns that the diversionary invasion in the Mohawk Valley has been given up.

SEPTEMBER 13–15. Burgoyne's army crosses to the west bank of the Hudson. The British make camp in the small town of Saratoga.

Gates's army advances to Bemis Heights, about ten miles south of Saratoga. Under the direction of the Polish engineer, Tadeusz Kosciuszko, work begins on a series of fortifications.

SEPTEMBER 15. The British army moves to Dovecot Heights.

SEPTEMBER 17. The redcoats advance two more miles.

SEPTEMBER 19. Burgoyne prepares to attack the Americans. He divides his army into three columns. The center column, under Burgoyne and General James Hamilton, is to march south on the heights. The right column, under General Simon Fraser, is to march inland to the west and then turn south to guard the right flank of the center column. The left column, of Germans under General Friedrich von Riedesel, will advance along the river road.

10:00–11:00 A.M. The British begin their march. Gates, learning of the enemy's movement, orders General Benedict Arnold to send out Colonel Daniel Morgan's Light Corps and support him with the rest of the left wing.

The British center and left columns halt to give Fraser time to get inland and make his turn to the south.

12:00–1:00 P.M. The redcoats resume their advance.

Pickets of the British center column, coming into the open fields at Freeman's farm, are fired on and decimated by Morgan's Light Corps. Hearing the sound of fighting, General Fraser sends troops running to the battlefield where the center column is forming into line. Morgan's men bump up against these forces. break, and retreat into the woods.

2:00 P.M. While Morgan re-forms his corps, Colonel Alexander Cilley's First New Hampshire Continentals attack the British right. After about twenty minutes of intense fighting, Cilley's troops withdraw, Dearborn's musketmen arriving too late to reinforce them. However, as they march back toward camp, Cilley's men are met by the Second and Third New Hampshire regiments, and they turn and rejoin the battle.

3:00 P.M. The fighting becomes general.

5:00 P.M. General Ebenezer Learned's brigade comes up and tries to swing around the British right; the move is unsuccessful. But the redcoats' center column is almost at the breaking point. The British artillery falls silent: all their ammunition is gone.

General Riedesel, on the River Road, receives orders from Burgoyne to strike the American right flank. Drums beating, the

Germans push inland to relieve the British from their desperate situation.

7:00–8:00 P.M. Gates's troops are battered by Riedesel's cannon, and the attack falters. At dusk, the Americans withdraw.

The losses: British—556 killed, wounded, or missing; American—299.

SEPTEMBER 20. The Americans nervously await the expected British attack. However it does not come: Burgoyne has decided to postpone it until September 21 to give his army a rest.

Gates informs the Continental Congress of the battle, giving credit for a victory to the American Army at large. Arnold's pride is wounded because Gates did not mention his name although all the American forces engaged in the battle were under his command.

SEPTEMBER 21. Burgoyne indefinitely postpones the planned attack on receipt of a letter from General Henry Clinton offering to make a diversionary attack at Fort Montgomery. Burgoyne answers immediately: "Do it, my dear friend, directly." (He overlooks the fact that at least two weeks will elapse before this can happen, and with reinforcements pouring into the American camp, time is on their side.)

SEPTEMBER 22. Gates transfers Morgan's Light Corps, formerly under Arnold, to his own command. Deeply insulted, Arnold writes a letter requesting a pass to leave the camp.

SEPTEMBER 23. Gates gives Arnold permission to leave. Arnold, not satisfied, writes Gates again saying that he wants an opportunity to defend himself against the "crimes" of which he has been accused. Gates answers that he has not insulted Arnold and encloses another pass, which Arnold refuses to use.

SEPTEMBER 25. Gates transfers Arnold's wing to his command and appoints General Benjamin Lincoln commander of the right wing. Arnold remains in camp without a command.

OCTOBER 4. Burgoyne holds a council of war in which he proposes a massive attack on Gates's left and rear. No decision is reached.

OCTOBER 5. When Burgoyne reconvenes his war council, General Riedesel proposes a retreat. Burgoyne makes a counterproposal: a probe of the American left on October 7 using 1500 regulars. If any weakness is found, the entire British army will attack on the 8th; if the Americans are too strong, the army will retreat. This plan is approved.

OCTOBER 7. 12:00 noon: The British advance begins.

1:00 P.M. After many stops to repair roads and bridge gullies for the artillery, the British column halts. Burgoyne's generals try to locate the enemy's camp but see only woods.

General Gates sends Colonel James Wilkinson out to reconnoitre the British position. When Wilkinson reports back, Gates orders him to send out Morgan's corps. Morgan suggests a wide sweep around the British right through the woods. Gates approves this plan. He orders Poor's brigade to strike the enemy's left while a part of Learned's brigade attacks the British center.

2:00–3:00 P.M. Poor's troops battle with the grenadiers guarding the redcoats' left flank.

Morgan strikes the enemy's right flank, scattering the British marksmen and other auxiliaries. The British Light Infantry forms to counterattack, but is stopped by the brutal fire of Major Henry Dearborn's musketmen. The British fall back, but rally a little to the rear. Burgoyne sends out orders for a retirement.

Learned's regiments attack the Germans in the British center. Arnold joins the assault, urging the Americans on. The Germans, although hard-pressed, hold their line until the withdrawal of the Light Infantry forces them to fall back.

The whole British line collapses with the arrival of General Abraham Ten Broeck's New York militia. The redcoats flee to their fortifications.

3:00 P.M. to dusk. Arnold leads an attack on the Balcarres redoubt around Freeman's farm, but the British repel each charge.

Elements of Learned's brigade capture two stockaded cabins near the Breymann redoubt. While some Americans attack the Breymann redoubt on the left center, the others strike the weak German force in the rear. The Germans flee in confusion as dusk falls. Darkness prevents the Americans from attacking the entirely unprotected British camp.

The losses: British killed, wounded, and missing—about 600; American—about 80.

OCTOBER 8. The British Army withdraws to a defensive position on the banks of the Hudson. In the evening the slow retreat north begins.

OCTOBER 9. By nightfall the British are at Saratoga.

OCTOBER 10. Burgoyne takes up a strong position with the Hudson to his east and the Fishkill to his south.

OCTOBER 12. Burgoyne decides to abandon his artillery and baggage and retreat by night. But at the last moment he realizes he has delayed too long: Gates's troops have completely surrounded his camp.

OCTOBER 13. The British agree to an honorable surrender.

OCTOBER 15. The articles of surrender are signed.

DECEMBER 4. France receives word of the American victory.

JANUARY 9, 1778. The American commissioners are informed that France will enter a treaty with the United States.

V

The BATTLES of SARATOGA– TWO HUNDRED YEARS LATER

TEN scant years separate us today from the bicentenary anniversary of the battles of Saratoga. Certain aspects of these encounters require a brief consideration from a historical point of view.

Why call them "The Battles of Saratoga"? They were not fought "at" Saratoga (now Schuylerville); the village of Stillwater was closer. At the time they were called "The Battles at Freeman's Farm" or "The Battles at Bemis Heights" or something similar. But the surrender was at Saratoga and it became common to speak of "The Victory of Saratoga," and "victory" carries the connotation of battles. When the United States government acquired the land on which the armies clashed and named it the "Saratoga National Historical Park," the battles in effect received an "official" title. Now it seems mere caviling to object to the term "The Battles of Saratoga."

History is merely a historian's attempt to reconstruct from various sources what happened in some era of the past. The Saratoga campaign was not over before the events began to be wrapped in myths, misrepresentations and falsehoods. These in turn have been added to by memoirs and secondary works until today it is impossible to give an account of the battles which will be accepted by all students of the events.

I believe the reader should be aware of my differences with many other writers.

I do not consider Burgoyne's plan for the invasion "grand on paper," "foolproof," and "a co-ordinated knockout blow." (The terms are used by several historians.) He never explained what was to be accomplished by the march and Germain never bothered to inquire. Most writers state that Howe was to march to Albany and some add a tale that Germain neglected to send the orders after they were written. The move would make Burgoyne's plan more understandable, but detailed studies now show that Howe was never ordered to Albany. Burgoyne's plan, combined with Howe's movement in the opposite direction by sea, marks a sad low point in British military planning.

Lack of space compelled me to do little more than to hint at the Schuyler-Gates controversy which is as alive today as it was when the two men lived. I have tried to be fair to both men, but I utterly reject as untenable the claim recently made that Schuyler deserves more credit than Gates for the defeat of Burgoyne.

Last—and most controversial—is Benedict Arnold's role in the battles. He was the fallen angel of the American

Revolution and, like Lucifer, has never lacked admirers and apologists. Intoxicated by the smell of gunpowder, he was a brave leader on horseback in battle. Inflated to heroic size, he was a demigod to Kenneth Roberts, the novelist whose books about the American Revolution have been most influential, and it is difficult to avoid believing that even some historians saw him in a romantic glow in order to give life to their texts. The visitor to the battle-fields comes away impressed by only one statue: the monument showing a boot and no name, an allusion to his wound and his treason.

I too would have preferred the romantic view of Arnold, but I am convinced from my study that most of it is fiction. Because of the controversy surrounding Arnold I concentrated my search principally to a critical examination of contemporary accounts and these are my conclusions:

1. There is no reliable evidence that Arnold led any attack in the first battle of Saratoga.

2. I found no contemporary evidence that Gates refused to send reinforcements to him during the first battle.

3. Arnold (by his own admission) was ordered by Gates to send out Morgan and to support him with the other units in his wing. This was what one would expect: the commanding general decided on the course of action and his subordinate carried out his plan.

4. Contrary to the careless assertions of some authors, Arnold did *not* complain in his famous letter to Gates of September 22, 1777, that Gates did not mention his leadership in the field during the first battle. As far as I can discover Arnold never claimed to have "led" the troops in this encounter.

5. In the second battle, no evidence was found to prove definitely when Arnold appeared on the battlefield aside from the fact he participated in the attack on the Balcarres redoubt. That he "led" the attack seems mere conjecture.

6. Arnold is often described as rallying his old Connecticut "neighbors" at this point. Actually the Connecticut regiment (Colonel Jonathan Lattimer's militia) was in Poor's brigade attacking the British left and not in the section of the field where Arnold appeared.

7. Although the evidence is not strong, it seems probable that the decision to attack the Breymann redoubt was made before Arnold appeared. All that is certain is that he joined an attack launched by Morgan's Light Corps, the Fifth and Sixth Massachusetts Continentals and other American troops against a redoubt held by a mere two hundred Germans. Whether Arnold helped to drive the Canadians from the stockaded cabins is dubious. Battle diagrams showing the Breymann redoubt being entered on the right side by Morgan and Arnold are in error.

8. I find little contemporary evidence to support the contention of Arnold's popularity with the simple soldiers of the American Army.

Probably few readers will have a chance to consult original sources to pass an independent judgment on the conclusions of an author. The best that can be desired is to encourage in the reader a healthy scepticism toward all written history and leave it to him to make his own choice.

If I found a "hero" in my study in whose favor I might be prejudiced, it was the common British or German soldier. These soldiers' extraordinary bravery in the face of overwhelming odds without any special incentive (the Americans were defending their homes and liberties), has rarely been noticed. In my opinion the battlefield at Saratoga National Historical Park will never be complete without a monument to these men.

FOR FURTHER READING

Nonfiction

ALDEN, JOHN RICHARD. *The American Revolution 1775–1783*. New York: Harper, 1962 (paperback).

ANBUREY, THOMAS. *With Burgoyne from Quebec*. Ed. by Sydney Jackman. Toronto: Macmillan of Canada, 1963.

BILLIAS, GEORGE A., ed. *George Washington's Generals*. New York: Morrow, 1964.

BIRD, HARRISON. *March to Saratoga*. New York: Oxford, 1963.

HAMILTON, EDWARD P. *Fort Ticonderoga*. Boston and Toronto: Little, Brown, 1964.

MONTROSS, LYNN. *Rag, Tag and Bobtail*. New York: Harper, 1952.

NICKERSON, HOFFMAN. *The Turning Point of the Revolution*. Boston: Houghton, Mifflin, 1928.

PETTENGILL, RAY W., trans. *Letters from America 1776–1779*. Port Washington, N.Y.: Kennikat Press, 1964.

SNELL, CHARLES W. and FRANCIS F. WILTSHIN. *Saratoga*. Washington, D.C.: Government Printing Office, 1961.

STANLEY, GEORGE F. G., ed. *For Want of a Horse*. Sackville, New Brunswick, Canada: Tribune Press, 1961.

WILCOX, WILLIAM B. *Portrait of a General*. New York: Knopf, 1964.

Fiction

GRAVES, ROBERT. *Sergeant Lamb's America*. New York: Random House, 1962 (paperback).

LANCASTER, BRUCE. *Guns of Burgoyne*. New York: Stokes, 1939.

ROBERTS, KENNETH. *Rabble in Arms*. New York: Doubleday, Doran, 1936 (also available in paperback).

INDEX